THE STORY OF SARAH MILLICAN

A Woman, Her Wit, and a Nation in Stitches

PAUL C. ANDREW

Copyright Page

Copyright [2023] [*PAUL C. ANDREW*]
All rights reserved. No part of this book may be reproduced in any form or by any electronic or mechanical means, including information storage and retrieval systems, without permission in writing from the publisher, except by a reviewer who may quote brief passages in a review.

The Information contained in this book is based on the author's experiences and research. The author has made every effort to provide accurate and up-to-date information, but makes no warranty or representation, express or implied, as to the accuracy or completeness of the information contained in this book. The author shall not be liable for any errors or omissions or for any actions taken based on the information contained in this book.

Table of Content

Introduction

Chapter 1: North East Roots

Chapter 2: The Road to Edinburgh

Chapter 3: Edinburgh Fringe Festival: Where Laughter Bloomed

Chapter 4: From Fringe to Fame: Television and the Spotlight

Chapter 5: Observational Queen: Making the Mundane Hilarious

Chapter 6: Breaking Barriers: A Voice for Women in Comedy

Chapter 7: Beyond the Stage: Books, Podcasts, and Creative Pursuits

Chapter 8: The Power of Laughter: Healing, Connection, and Social Commentary

Chapter 9: Legacy and Influence: Inspiring a New Generation of Comedians

Chapter 10: The Future of Wit: Where Laughter Takes Her Next

Epilogue: A Nation in Stitches: Sarah Millican's Laughter Revolution

Introduction

Imagine a roomful of strangers, faces creased with laughter, bellies aching from the sheer absurdity of it all. In the center, bathed in the warm glow of the spotlight, stands a woman with a mischievous glint in her eye and a microphone cradled in her hand. This is Sarah Millican, queen of the observational quip, weaver of wit, and the woman who single-handedly stitched an entire nation into one laughing, snorting, tear-wiping mess.

Her story isn't one of meteoric rise and overnight fame. It's a journey of grit, vulnerability, and the slow burn of finding her voice, a voice that would resonate from smoky comedy clubs to sold-out arenas, making friends along the way with supermarket check-out ladies, shy teenagers, and everyone in between.

This book is more than a biography; it's a love letter to laughter, a testament to the transformative power of humor. It delves into the fertile soil of Sarah's North East roots, where humor bloomed amidst shipyard sirens and family gatherings. We trace her path from shy girl to budding comedienne, navigating the crucible of open mic nights and the electrifying highs and soul-crushing lows of the Edinburgh Fringe Festival.

Beyond the punchlines, we explore the woman behind the wit. We witness her championing of relatable comedy, her fearless voice breaking down barriers for women in humor, and her #JoinIn initiative, a beacon of community and support for those wrestling with life's absurdities.

But Sarah Millican's brilliance lies not just in making us laugh, but in making us think. She holds a mirror to our everyday lives, magnifying the hilarious mundaneness of it all, turning mundane chores and social awkwardness into comedic gold. Her humor becomes a weapon against cynicism, a shield against loneliness, and a bridge connecting us to the shared fabric of our human experience.

So, turn the page and step into the world of Sarah Millican. Prepare to laugh until your sides ache, to be moved by her honesty, and to discover the transformative power of humor that can stitch together not just a roomful of strangers, but a nation in stitches.

Chapter 1: North East Roots

Laughing in the Shipyards: A Childhood Shaped by Humor and Resilience

Born in South Shields, England, on May 29th, 1975, Sarah Millican wasn't destined for the spotlight. Her childhood wasn't gilded with privilege; it was etched in the gritty, industrial landscape of a working-class town where humor wasn't a luxury, but a lifeline. The clang of the shipyards, the salty tang of the North Sea, and the warmth of close-knit communities formed the backdrop against which Sarah's wit took its first, wobbly steps.

Laughter wasn't just a sound in Sarah's childhood; it was a language. It danced on the lips of her shipyard-working father, seasoned with tales of camaraderie and the occasional mishap. It echoed in the kitchen, where her mother, a master storyteller, spun yarns that stretched from the mundane to the fantastical, always leaving a trail of giggles in their wake. Humor wasn't a performance; it was woven into the fabric of family life, a shared currency that bought comfort in tough times and amplified joy in good ones.

Life in South Shields wasn't always sunshine and laughter. The economic tides ebbed and flowed, casting shadows on the family's finances. Yet, even in the face of hardship, the Millicans clung to their sense of humor. Sarah, a shy child with a watchful eye, absorbed the resilience and wit around her. She learned to find amusement in the everyday, to turn a dropped egg into a slapstick routine and a rainy day into an excuse for an indoor pillow fight.

Beyond the home, Sarah's North East roots offered a vibrant tapestry of characters and situations ripe for comedic fodder. The eccentricities of her neighbors, the quirks of local shopkeepers, and the unspoken rules of schoolyard hierarchies provided endless material for her budding observational skills. She found humor in the mundane, the awkward, and the downright bizarre, a skill that would later blossom into her trademark brand of observational comedy.

But Sarah's journey wasn't without its challenges. Her shyness often masked her quick wit, making it difficult to share her humor with the world. Yet, even in the quiet corners of her childhood, her mind crackled with creativity. She wrote poems in secret, whispered jokes to her pets, and filled notebooks with stories that hinted at the comedic genius waiting to unleash.

In the laughter-soaked streets of South Shields, Sarah Millican didn't just find her voice; she discovered a resilience that would become the foundation of her comedic persona. The North East, with its gritty charm and unflinching humor, provided the stage where she learned to laugh in the face of adversity, find humor in the everyday, and, one day, take that laughter to the nation and stitch it together in stitches.

This is just the beginning of Sarah Millican's story, a tale of laughter, resilience, and the transformative power of humor. Turn the page and step into the world of this North East wit, where the echoes of shipyard sirens and family laughter mingle with the promise of a future filled with side-splitting stand-up and a nation in stitches.

Finding Her Voice: From Shy Girl to Budding Comedienne

Sarah Millican's roots weren't planted in the glamour of London's West End, but in the gritty realism of North Shields, England. A working-class town etched by shipyard sirens and industrial chimneys, it was an unlikely breeding ground for a comedic queen. Yet, amidst the rust and resilience, the seeds of Sarah's humor were sown.

Growing up, she wasn't the life of the party, not the girl who commanded attention with booming laughter or sparkling wit. Instead, she was quietly observant, soaking in the eccentricities of her family and neighborhood like a sponge. Her father, a welder with a penchant for deadpan delivery, became her first comedic muse, peppering their everyday lives with dry remarks and playful jabs. Her mother, a woman of sharp wit and unspoken strength, instilled in Sarah a keen eye for the absurd, teaching her to find humor in the mundane, the unexpected, the "well, that went swimmingly" moments of life.

But within young Sarah simmered a shy reserve. Public speaking was a hurdle, a mountain to be climbed with a quivering voice and clammy palms. Yet, there was a spark, a glimmer of comedic rebellion that refused to be extinguished. It flickered in family gatherings, ignited by a well-timed observation or a mischievous mimicry of an aunt's laugh. At school, it emerged in the safety of anonymity, scribbling witty captions on classmates' photos or crafting satirical plays performed only for the stage of her imagination.

The turning point came, as with so many things, through sheer necessity. After graduating with a degree in drama, Sarah found herself adrift in a sea of uncertainty. With acting jobs scarce and the world seemingly closed to her introverted nature, she stumbled upon the open mic night at The Stand comedy club in Newcastle. It was a baptism by laughter, a baptism by nerves. Stepping onto that stage for the first time, microphone cold and spotlight unforgiving, Sarah felt every fiber of her being scream in protest. Yet, she pushed through, channeling her anxieties into self-deprecating jokes and observations of the awkward realities of young adulthood.

The laughter that met her was like a jolt of electricity. It wasn't just the validation, though that was certainly present. It was the discovery of a power she never knew she possessed: the power to transform her shyness into something relatable, something universally funny. From that night on, the timid girl from North Shields began to morph into the budding comedian, finding her voice through the microphone and her confidence amidst the clatter of pint glasses and the applause of strangers.

This journey from the quiet observer to the blossoming performer wasn't a linear rise to fame. It was a series of stumbles and stutters, setbacks and small victories. But in each moment, Sarah honed her craft, her observational humor finding its focus, her self-deprecating charm winning over audiences. She began building her repertoire, mining the fertile ground of her North East upbringing, the family dinners, the rain-swept streets, the eccentricities of working-class life, turning them into comedic nuggets that resonated with a truth both specific and universal.

By the time Sarah left the shores of North Shields for the wider stage of Edinburgh, she wasn't just a comedian; she was a storyteller, a weaver of laughter from the fabric of her own life. And it was this authenticity, this deep connection to her roots, that would become the cornerstone of her comedic empire, the very foundation of her journey from shy girl to the woman who would one day make a nation cry with laughter.

Chapter 2: The Road to Edinburgh

Stand-Up Beginnings: Taking the Stage and Facing Fears

The flickering glow of a dim pub mic, the expectant faces huddled in the darkness, the silence broken only by the clinking of glasses – this was Sarah Millican's baptism by fire. Her journey to comedy wasn't a flash of inspiration, but a slow, intrepid climb, each hesitant step onto a dingy stage a victory over an ocean of fears.

Before the laughter, there was trepidation. Armed with jokes scribbled on scraps of paper and a heart pounding like a hummingbird on Red Bull, she would navigate the treacherous shoals of open mic nights. The early years were a baptism by embarrassment. Jokes misfired, audiences shuffled awkwardly, and silence, heavier than a dropped pie, descended like a judgmental fog. Yet, through it all, Sarah clung to a stubborn streak of wit and a determination to make people laugh.

She honed her craft in the crucible of comedy clubs, learning to read audiences like tea leaves, adjusting her material to the ebb and flow of laughter. Every bombed joke was a lesson learned, every awkward pause a brick laid in the foundation of her comedic confidence. She discovered the power of self-deprecation, transforming nervousness into relatable charm. Her humor, rooted in the everyday – the awkward dates, the domestic mishaps, the relatable anxieties – resonated with audiences who saw themselves reflected in her self-deprecating wit.

Edinburgh, the holy grail of comedy, loomed as both a dream and a daunting Everest. The festival, a whirlwind of auditions, performances, and ruthless reviews, could make or break careers. To stand on that stage meant confronting not just audiences, but self-doubt, a monstrous dragon guarding the gates of comedic legitimacy.

In 2005, with more grit than glitter, Sarah took the plunge. Her debut Edinburgh show, "Not Nice," wasn't polished or perfect. It was raw, honest, and utterly relatable. She talked about heartbreak, awkward sex, and the indignities of public toilets with a self-aware humor that had audiences cackling in recognition. While not an overnight sensation, the show garnered critical acclaim and, more importantly, the confidence to keep climbing.

Sarah Millican's stand-up beginnings were a testament to the transformative power of perseverance. She battled nerves, navigated rejection, and embraced the awkwardness of finding her voice. This early chapter, rife with both stumbles and successes, laid the foundation for the comedic powerhouse she would become, proving that laughter, like courage, can be forged in the fires of fear.

Hone Your Craft: The Crucible of Comedy Clubs and Open Mics

The Edinburgh Fringe Festival might be the holy grail, but the path to that comedic Mecca is paved with the blood, sweat, and questionable jokes of open mic nights and fledgling comedy clubs. For

Sarah Millican, this was the fertile ground where her raw comedic talent met the brutal realities of stage time. It was a baptism by fire, a forge where the steel of her jokes was tempered, reshaped, and occasionally shattered to be welded anew.

Imagine a smoky room tucked away above a pub, reeking of stale beer and nervous anticipation. That's the breeding ground for the next generation of funny, where seasoned comics rub shoulders with wide-eyed newcomers like Sarah. The stage, bathed in the harsh glare of a single spotlight, became her classroom, every heckle a pop quiz, every bomb a failed experiment. Nights flew by in a blur of nervous sweat, forgotten punchlines, and the occasional unexpected laugh that crackled in the air like a lightning bolt, confirming that maybe, just maybe, she was onto something.

These weren't nights for polish or perfection. They were for testing jokes in the furnace of audience reactions, witnessing what landed and what went up in smoke. Sarah honed her observational humor, crafting relatable routines from the minutiae of everyday life – navigating awkward family gatherings, the trials of supermarket queues, the eternal battle against rogue tights. Laughter became her currency, and she learned to read the room like a seasoned gambler, adjusting her delivery, tweaking her timing, always searching for that sweet spot where the mundane met the hilarious.

Open mics weren't just about laughs, though. They were a baptism by heckle, a crash course in comedic resilience. The occasional heckler, loud and uninvited, would become a sparring partner, forcing Sarah to think on her feet, to improvise, to turn heckles into comedic fodder. These tests forged her quick wit, sharpened her reflexes, and instilled in her an unflinching stage presence.

But the journey wasn't all punchlines and put-downs. There were nights of silence, rooms that died a slow death under the weight of unfunny jokes. Doubt gnawed at her, whispering its poisonous questions: "Is this good enough?" "Are you kidding yourself?" Yet, through it all, she persevered, driven by a quiet, stubborn determination. Each failed joke was a lesson learned, each awkward silence a stepping stone on the path to her own comedic voice.

The crucible of open mics and comedy clubs was more than just honing her craft. It was forging an identity. It was where Sarah, the shy girl from the North East, transformed into Sarah Millican, the comedian. It was where she discovered the transformative power of laughter, not just for herself, but for the strangers who packed into rooms to share in her journey. And it was the preparation she needed, the armor she forged, to take on the Edinburgh Fringe, the ultimate test of her comedic mettle.

So, the next time you hear Sarah Millican deliver a perfectly timed quip, remember the journey that came before. Remember the smoky rooms, the nervous sweat, the laughter and the silence. Remember the woman who honed her craft in the crucible of comedy clubs and open mics, the woman who dared to make us laugh at ourselves, and in doing so, stitched together a community of shared moments and uproarious joy.

Chapter 3: Edinburgh Fringe Festival: Where Laughter Bloomed

The Breakthrough: A Newcomer Takes the Fringe by Storm

Edinburgh in August. The cobbled streets thrum with anticipation, a vibrant circus of street performers and flyers buzzing like overstimulated bees. And amidst this whirlwind, Sarah Millican, a then-unknown comic from the north east, was about to step onto a stage and change her life. It wasn't just a performance; it was a baptism by laughter, a moment where a shy woman became a comedic force.

Her show, "Sarah Millican's Not Nice," wasn't about punchlines and callbacks. It was raw, honest, and deeply personal. She mined the humor from the wreckage of her recent divorce, her vulnerabilities laid bare on stage like an offering to the comedy gods. It was relatable, messy, and refreshingly unfiltered. This wasn't a polished routine; it was a conversation with the audience, a shared journey through the absurdities of heartbreak and self-discovery.

And the audience laughed. They roared with laughter, a wave of collective release washing over the room. They recognized themselves in her words – the awkward silences, the messy emotions, the dark humor bubbling beneath the surface of ordinary life. Millican wasn't just making jokes; she was giving voice to the unspoken, the universal ache of human experience.

But it wasn't just the honesty that resonated. It was her delivery. A dry wit laced with an endearing vulnerability, a mischievous glint in her eyes that hinted at the chaos lurking beneath the surface. She possessed a quiet confidence, an unassuming swagger that somehow commanded the stage. She wasn't just telling jokes; she was weaving a tapestry of humor, personal truths, and unexpected observations, holding the audience captive with every twist and turn.

Word spread like wildfire through the cramped corridors of the Fringe. "Not Nice" wasn't just a show; it was a buzzword, a whispered promise of laughter and a glimpse of truth. Critics, usually jaded by an endless parade of hopefuls, sat up and took notice. Reviewers lauded her honesty, her originality, and her undeniable comedic talent. Awards nominations followed, whispers of "Best Newcomer" swirling around her like a benevolent fog.

The culmination came on a balmy Edinburgh evening, the air thick with anticipation. The announcement of the Best Newcomer award echoed through the packed room, each beat of silence building the tension. And then, her name. Sarah Millican, the shy woman from the north east, the one who dared to be honest and funny about divorce and lady gardens, had conquered the Fringe.

That night wasn't just about winning an award; it was a turning point. It was the moment Sarah Millican, the comedian, bloomed. The laughter of the audience, the validation of the critics, the echo of her own name – they were all seeds sown, promising a harvest of comedy yet to come. Her story, raw and real, had found its rhythm, its audience, and its voice. And from the cobbled streets of Edinburgh, a nation-wide ripple of laughter was about to begin.

From Recognition to Revelation: Finding Her Authentic Voice

The spotlight pulsed like a beating heart, throwing long shadows across the makeshift stage. Laughter had already washed over the audience, leaving them breathless and expectant. Taking a deep breath, Sarah Millican stepped forward, her mic stand casting a silhouette against the flickering lights. This was it – the Fringe, the crucible where careers were forged and reputations made. This wasn't just another Edinburgh night; it was the precipice towards a new future.

Recognition had come swiftly after her "Newcomer" award win. Television appearances beckoned, audiences grew larger, and the pressure mounted. But somewhere amidst the whirlwind, Sarah felt a dissonant note in her performance. The material, sharp and clever, resonated with audiences, but it felt borrowed, not genuinely her own. On the Fringe stage, with its raw intimacy and unforgiving honesty, the mask faltered.

The early shows were a rollercoaster. The familiar routines landed, eliciting familiar bursts of laughter. But then, amidst the prepared anecdotes, Sarah slipped in a personal story, a whispered observation about her divorce, the vulnerability raw and exposed. The laughter that followed was different, tinged with empathy and recognition. In that moment, a fissure opened in the carefully constructed persona, revealing a depth that resonated beyond the punchlines.

It wasn't a conscious decision, but a subtle shift. More personal stories weaved their way into the set, tales of everyday anxieties and awkward encounters, delivered with self-deprecating humor and a disarming honesty. The laughter deepened, laced with a sense of shared humanity.

Sarah wasn't just making the audience laugh; she was laughing with them, inviting them into a world where the messy realities of life could be met with humor and acceptance.

The reviews, once impressed but reserved, began to sing a different tune. Critics lauded her authenticity, her ability to find humor in the universal quirks of being human. Audiences flocked back, drawn to the woman who dared to laugh at life's absurdities, her own included. By the end of the Fringe, Sarah wasn't just a comedian; she was a revelation, a voice whispering, "It's okay to be you, laugh at your own stumbles, and find joy in the ordinary."

The Edinburgh Fringe had become more than a springboard to fame; it was a mirror reflecting her back, not an idealized version, but the real Sarah, flaws and all. And in that reflection, she discovered her most potent weapon – her own unapologetic authenticity. This Edinburgh wasn't just about recognition; it was about revelation, a stepping stone on a journey towards a humor that would not only make people laugh, but also bring them closer to themselves and each other, stitches not just for broken jokes, but for the broken bits of life we all carry.

Chapter 4: From Fringe to Fame: Television and the Spotlight

Live at the Apollo and Beyond: Embracing the National Stage

The Edinburgh Fringe had been a crucible, forging Sarah Millican's raw talent into a polished gem. But the stage lights dimmed, the applause faded, and the question loomed: where next? The answer, as fate would have it, blinked brightly on the national television screen.

In 2008, Sarah landed a coveted spot on "Live at the Apollo," the legendary platform that had launched countless comedic careers. The pressure was palpable, the audience a sea of unfamiliar faces. Yet, Sarah took the stage with the same disarmingly honest charm that had captivated Edinburgh. She spoke of the trials of bra fittings, the joys of solitude, the absurdities of everyday life – her humor resonating with a universality that transcended regional borders. Laughter rippled through the theater, a chorus of recognition that washed over Sarah like a warm wave. She had conquered not just the stage, but a new audience, proving her appeal stretched far beyond the Fringe's bohemian enclave.

"Live at the Apollo" was just the beginning. Panel shows like "QI" and "Mock the Week" eagerly welcomed Sarah's sharp wit and observational eye. She became a regular guest, her dry delivery and self-deprecating humor adding a unique flavor to the comedic cocktail. On "Have I Got News for You," she fearlessly tackled the absurdities of politics, proving that her humor wasn't afraid to tread where angels fear to joke.

But Sarah wasn't content to be a guest star. In 2008, she landed her own sitcom, "The Sarah Millican Show." The show was a love letter to the everyday, a hilarious window into the life of a woman navigating awkward dates, eccentric family members, and the existential anxieties of living in a world obsessed with Ikea furniture. It wasn't just funny; it was real. Sarah wasn't afraid to be vulnerable, to laugh at her own flaws and insecurities, creating a character audiences could truly connect with.

"The Sarah Millican Show" was a critical and commercial success, cementing Sarah's place in the national comedic landscape. She was no longer just a Fringe favorite; she was a household name, her face gracing magazine covers and her voice filling airwaves. The shy girl from South Shields had become a comedy queen, her wit a beacon of laughter in the often-dreary landscape of everyday life.

But with fame came a new challenge: navigating the spotlight. Sarah, ever the champion of the ordinary, refused to be consumed by celebrity. She remained grounded, her humor retaining its relatable edge. She eschewed the glossy world of red carpets for supermarket aisles, her audience not just celebrities but the checkout ladies, the dog walkers, the working mothers who found solace in her humor.

Sarah's success wasn't just about her; it was about a shift in the comedic landscape. She paved the way for a new generation of women in comedy, proving that humor didn't have to be loud or brash to be effective. Her observational wit, her vulnerability, and her utter disregard for the "funny girl" stereotype made her a role model, a champion of the relatable and the real.

So, as the applause died down on the "Live at the Apollo" stage, it wasn't just the end of a show, it was the beginning of a national love affair with a comedian who had dared to be herself, to laugh at life's absurdities, and, in doing so, to stitch together a nation in stitches. Sarah Millican had crossed the threshold from Fringe favorite to national treasure, proving that sometimes, the funniest stories are the ones we all share.

The Sarah Millican Show: Creating a Comedy Empire

Emerging from the Edinburgh Fringe's applause-drenched haze, Sarah Millican stood poised at the precipice of a new frontier:

television. Her sharp wit and relatable observations had already conquered festival crowds, but could they translate to the wider gaze of the national screen? The answer, delivered with a trademark wry smile, was an emphatic "Absolutely, darling."

In 2008, "The Sarah Millican Show" premiered on BBC Two, bursting onto the scene like a comedic firework, vibrant and unexpected. No longer confined to stand-up routines, Sarah wove her humor into a tapestry of sketches, characterizations, and observational gold. She was the everywoman at the supermarket checkout, the exasperated sister at a chaotic Christmas dinner, the voice giving life to the unspoken thoughts bubbling beneath the surface of British life.

The show was an instant hit. Critics, long starved of fresh comedic voices, hailed it as a breath of fresh air. Audiences, previously accustomed to sitcoms with exaggerated scenarios and canned laughter, flocked to Sarah's world of relatable humor and honest vulnerability. Ratings soared, awards clinked, and "The Sarah Millican Show" became a cultural phenomenon.

But Sarah's empire wasn't built on mere mimicry of existing sitcoms. Her genius lay in taking the mundane and making it hilariously extraordinary. A trip to the dentist became a surreal odyssey of fear and awkwardness, a visit to the gym morphed into a slapstick ballet of flailing limbs and misplaced lycra. No topic, from periods to pubic hair, was deemed too taboo for her wry observation and self-deprecating humor.

Beyond the laughter, "The Sarah Millican Show" offered a safe space for honest conversations about womanhood, relationships, and the messy joy of being human. Sarah was the friend confiding secrets over a cup of tea, the sister-in-arms sharing relatable struggles, the aunt chuckling at life's absurdities. She created a community of laughter, where women could recognize themselves in every awkward giggle and heartfelt sentiment.

However, Sarah's reign as queen of comedic television wasn't without its challenges. The pressure to constantly outdo her previous success weighed heavily, and the relentless media scrutiny tested her resilience. Yet, she faced it all with the same unflinching honesty and self-deprecating humor that endeared her to audiences.

Ultimately, "The Sarah Millican Show" became more than just a sitcom; it was a testament to the power of relatable humor, a celebration of women's voices in comedy, and a heartwarming reminder that in the shared absurdities of everyday life, there's always a reason to laugh. It cemented Sarah Millican's place not just as a successful comedian, but as a comedic pioneer, paving the way for a generation of women to find their voices and conquer the stage with unflinching honesty and laughter.

As the curtains closed on the final episode of "The Sarah Millican Show" in 2010, it wasn't the end of an era, but the beginning of a comedic empire still to be fully explored. Sarah's humor had resonated, her laughter had echoed, and the nation remained in stitches, eager to see what her wit would weave next.

Chapter 5: Observational Queen: Making the Mundane Hilarious

Life's Little Laughs: Finding Humor in the Everyday

Sarah Millican's magic lies not in fantastical tales or outlandish characters, but in the quiet corners of our own lives. She's the master of the mundane, the alchemizer of the everyday, the one who turns supermarket checkouts, awkward family dinners, and the existential dread of a Tuesday afternoon into pure comedic gold. Her jokes aren't about escaping reality; they're about embracing it, laughing at its absurdities, and finding the hidden humor in the wrinkles of our shared experience.

Millican's comedy thrives on relatable details. She doesn't shy away from the unglamorous, the awkward, the slightly embarrassing aspects of life. We recognize ourselves in her characters – the woman struggling with a rogue bra strap in public, the one who loses her keys in the most ridiculous places, the one who contemplates the existential angst of choosing the right avocado. This isn't stand-up as self-aggrandizement; it's a shared laugh, a knowing wink that says, "Yes, I've been there too, and isn't it just absurdly hilarious?"

The mundane becomes the canvas for her observational brilliance. She elevates the mundane to the hilarious by zooming in, highlighting the absurdities that might otherwise slip unnoticed. A trip to the dentist becomes a meditation on the existential horror of open mouths and drool. A journey down the biscuit aisle becomes a comedic battle royale between digestive responsibility and pure, unadulterated temptation. A conversation with a particularly chirpy checkout operator becomes a linguistic odyssey through the land of insincere pleasantries.

Millican's humor isn't just funny; it's disarmingly honest. She doesn't pretend to have life figured out; she embraces the messiness, the contradictions, the hilarious imperfections. She laughs at her own anxieties, insecurities, and bodily functions, inviting us to do the same. This vulnerability becomes a bridge, connecting us to her and to each other, reminding us that we're not alone in our absurd, hilarious human experience.

More than just a laugh, Millican's humor offers a kind of validation. It tells us that the ordinary, the mundane, the slightly embarrassing bits of our lives are not only worthy of attention, but they are also inherently funny. It's a permission slip to laugh at ourselves, to find joy in the everyday, and to recognize that even the most mundane moments hold the potential for comedic gold.

So, the next time you find yourself stuck in a supermarket queue, dreading the dentist appointment, or contemplating the existential dilemma of choosing the right avocado, remember Sarah Millican. Remember that laughter is always there, waiting to be mined from the everyday, ready to stitch together our shared experience into a tapestry of hilarious absurdity. And who knows, maybe you'll even discover your own inner observational comedian, ready to find the humor in the mundane and laugh your way through life.

Championing the Relatable: Connecting with Audiences Through Shared Experiences

Sarah Millican isn't your typical stand-up comedian, dissecting the absurdities of politics or the existential dread of modern life. Instead, she wields a magnifying glass, zooming in on the microscopic imperfections of our everyday existence, transforming the mundane into side-splitting material. Supermarket queues, awkward first dates, the utter bewilderment of flat-pack furniture – these are the battlegrounds of her comedic conquests.

Millican's genius lies in her ability to see the humor in the universal. She delves into the shared experiences that bind us, the embarrassing moments, the unspoken anxieties, the quirks and foibles that make us human. Whether it's the struggle to navigate a crowded bus with a overflowing shopping bag, the existential crisis of choosing the right type of lettuce, or the sheer terror of parallel parking, she holds a mirror to our collective soul, reflecting back the hilarious absurdity of it all.

Her comedy isn't a distant, intellectual exercise; it's a warm, inviting hug, a knowing wink that says, "Hey, you're not alone in this." We recognize ourselves in her tales of wardrobe malfunctions, social faux pas, and the daily battle against the tyranny of technology. We laugh not at her, but with her, a shared chorus of recognition echoing through the auditorium.

Millican's strength lies in her unflinching honesty. She doesn't shy away from the awkward, the embarrassing, the messy realities of life. She speaks of cellulite and periods with the same casual frankness as she talks about the weather, stripping away the shame and stigma that often surround these topics, particularly for women. In doing so, she creates a space where vulnerability is strength, where laughter is a bridge across the chasms of insecurity and self-doubt.

By championing the relatable, Millican becomes not just a comedian, but a confidante, a friend who whispers in our ear, "It's okay to be weird, it's okay to be clumsy, it's okay to be human." And in that whispered reassurance, we find not just amusement, but a sense of belonging, a reminder that we're all in this hilarious, messy, magnificent journey together.

For in the quiet corners of our everyday lives, there's a whole universe of humor waiting to be discovered, a universe where even the most mundane moments can become side-splitting odes to the human condition.

Chapter 6: Breaking Barriers: A Voice for Women in Comedy

Challenging Stereotypes: Redefining Comedy and Representation

Sarah Millican wasn't just another funny woman on stage. She was a seismic shift, a tectonic plate in the landscape of stand-up comedy. For too long, the humor industry had been a boys' club, echoing with laddish jokes and one-dimensional female characters. But Sarah entered, not with a crowbar, but with a wry smile and a laser-sharp wit, ready to dismantle stereotypes brick by brick.

Her humor was decidedly un-ladylike. Gone were the predictable routines about hair extensions and shopping sprees. Instead, Sarah delved into the darker, messier corners of womanhood—periods, body hair, the tyranny of tights—with a frankness that was both hilarious and disarming. She dared to be unapologetically human, to laugh at her own imperfections, and in doing so, gave permission for a generation of women to do the same.

But Sarah's impact went beyond mere content. She challenged the very structure of the comedy world. In an industry dominated by male gatekeepers, she carved her own path, creating her own sitcom, writing her own material, and refusing to conform to the tired tropes of female comedians. She became a beacon for aspiring women, proving that humor wasn't a gendered gift, but a universal language anyone could wield.

Her influence extended beyond the stage, too. Sarah's #JoinIn initiative, a social media campaign encouraging people to share stories of kindness and laughter, became a testament to the power of humor to bridge divides and build communities. It was a space for women, often marginalized in the public sphere, to find their voices, share their experiences, and ultimately, laugh at themselves and each other.

Of course, Sarah's journey wasn't without its bumps. She faced criticism for being "too outspoken," for pushing the boundaries of what was considered "appropriate" female humor. But she never wavered. Her humor, born from honesty and vulnerability, resonated with audiences who saw themselves reflected in her unapologetic self-deprecation. They saw a woman who dared to be funny without shrinking herself, who embraced the messy, hilarious reality of being female in a world that often tried to silence them.

In the end, Sarah Millican's legacy isn't just about the jokes, though they were undeniably brilliant. It's about the doors she opened, the voices she amplified, and the laughter that served as a powerful tool for dismantling stereotypes and redefining what it meant to be a woman, a comedian, and a human being in the face of life's absurdities. She showed us that humor could be a weapon, a shield, and a bridge—and in doing so, she left the comedy world, and the world at large, a little bit funnier, a little bit braver, and a whole lot more stitched together.

#JoinIn: Stitching Laughter, Not Seams

In the annals of comedy, the landscape was once bleak for women. Stereotyped as shrill housewives or giggling sidekicks, their voices rarely held the stage with the same authority and freedom as their male counterparts. Enter Sarah Millican, a disruptor with a razor-sharp wit and a heart the size of a Tyne Bridge. Her comedy dared to be different, refusing to conform to the tired tropes of female humor. She spoke of periods and menopause, body hair and bad relationships, not with coy euphemisms or nervous giggles, but with a bold, unflinching honesty that resonated deeply with women who had yearned to see themselves reflected on stage, imperfections and all.

But Sarah's impact went beyond mere representation. She became a beacon of support, building a community of laughter and connection through her #JoinIn initiative. What began as a simple gesture – urging those spending Christmas alone to tweet and find company – blossomed into a vibrant online gathering. The hashtag became a lifeline, a virtual pub full of warm wit and open arms. Sharing funny anecdotes, offering words of comfort, and simply being present for each other, the #JoinIn community thrived, proving that laughter could be a powerful anti-isolation serum.

Sarah's own openness about her struggles with depression and anxiety further cemented her role as a champion of vulnerability. She spoke candidly about her mental health, not as a punchline, but as a shared human experience. In doing so, she normalized conversations about mental well-being, reminding us that even the funniest folks can have blue days. This vulnerability became a bridge, allowing others to find comfort in shared experiences and seek help without shame.

The #JoinIn movement transcended the digital realm, spilling over into charity work and live events. Sarah, ever the champion of the underdog, hosted fundraising events for mental health charities and organized live Christmas Day gatherings for those who wouldn't be alone. The laughter at these events wasn't just an escape, it was a statement: a community stitched together by humor, empathy, and the knowledge that no one needs to face life's absurdities alone.

Ultimately, Sarah Millican's impact on women in comedy is multifaceted. She broke down barriers with her unapologetic humor, paved the way for a new generation of female comics, and built a community where laughter served as a shield against loneliness and a compass towards connection. #JoinIn became more than just a hashtag; it became a testament to the unifying power of shared vulnerability and the strength found in laughter's embrace.

With #JoinIn, Sarah Millican stitched together not just jokes, but a tapestry of compassion, reminding us that even the darkest laughter can light the way towards a brighter, more connected future.

Chapter 7: Beyond the Stage: Books, Podcasts, and Creative Pursuits

From Stand-Up to Sit-Down: Sharing Her Story in Print

While Sarah Millican's onstage persona thrived on spontaneity and wit, a yearning for something more permanent stirred within her. In 2017, this desire materialized in the form of her debut book, "How to be Champion." Part autobiography, part self-help guide, and all parts hilarious, the book wasn't just a literary extension of her comedic persona; it was a heartfelt exploration of her life, vulnerabilities, and triumphs.

Millican didn't shy away from the raw realities of navigating life as a woman in comedy. She delved into the self-doubt, the challenges of finding her voice, and the bittersweet reality of balancing success with vulnerability. Her prose crackled with the same wit that lit up stages, but there was an added depth, a sense of intimacy that invited readers into her world beyond the punchlines.

"How to be Champion" wasn't just a comedic romp; it was a relatable roadmap for anyone navigating life's twists and turns. Millican offered humorous nuggets of wisdom gleaned from personal experience, tackling topics like body image, relationships, and the quest for self-acceptance. She turned everyday anxieties into laugh-out-loud anecdotes, reminding readers that vulnerability can be hilarious, relatable, and ultimately, empowering.

The book's success further cemented Millican's status as a multifaceted creative force. It wasn't just a one-off venture, either. Her foray into the written word became another platform for her wit and wisdom. Articles, essays, and guest columns followed, each adding another layer to the tapestry of her creative output.

But Millican's creative itch continued to scratch. In 2021, she launched "Standard Issue," a magazine-style podcast co-hosted with friend and producer, Susan Calman. The podcast wasn't just another celebrity chatter show. It was a vibrant, unapologetically female-focused space for honest conversations about life, love, and the hilarious absurdities of everyday existence.

Through "Standard Issue," Millican proved that her storytelling prowess wasn't confined to the stage or the page. She fostered a community where women could laugh, share, and connect, celebrating the messy, imperfect realities of their lives. Interviews with inspiring guests, from writers and comedians to scientists and activists, furthered the podcast's reach, creating a platform for diverse voices and perspectives.

Ultimately, Sarah Millican's ventures beyond stand-up were not departures, but expansions. They were testaments to her insatiable curiosity, her desire to connect with her audience on a deeper level, and her willingness to explore new avenues for her comedic genius. Whether it was through the intimate vulnerability of her book, the vibrant conversations of her podcast, or the insightful explorations of her essays, Millican continued to share her voice, stitching together communities of laughter and leaving her mark far beyond the confines of the stage.

Standard Issue: Exploring Life, Laughter, and Everything In-Between

While Sarah Millican's stand-up remained her primary canvas, her creative spirit yearned for wider horizons. In 2014, she co-founded Standard Issue, an online magazine for women. Unlike the glossy, airbrushed ideal often peddled by mainstream publications, Standard Issue embraced the diverse tapestry of female experience. It was a platform for relatable women's voices, celebrating the messy, authentic, and often hilarious realities of life.

From hilarious essays on IBS to candid discussions about aging and relationships, Standard Issue resonated with women who felt ignored by the mainstream. It was a safe space to laugh at the absurdities of life, share vulnerabilities, and connect over shared experiences. Sarah herself was an active contributor, her sharp wit and honest observations adding a unique blend of humor and warmth to the platform.

However, the magazine's financial realities proved challenging. In 2017, with a heavy heart, Sarah announced its closure. Yet, the spirit of Standard Issue refused to be silenced. In 2016, it metamorphosed into a weekly podcast, aptly titled "Standard Issue." The format shifted, but the essence remained – a vibrant community of women, united by laughter and a shared pursuit of authenticity.

The podcast became a platform for Sarah to explore beyond the confines of stand-up. Interviews with inspirational women, from comedians to politicians, offered audiences a glimpse into diverse perspectives and experiences. Discussions on everything from body image to grief provided a safe space for open conversation and shared vulnerabilities. In a world often obsessed with curated online personas, Sarah's podcast embraced the rawness and complexity of being human.

But Sarah's creative pursuits weren't limited to words. In 2017, she penned her first book, "How to Be Champion." Blending humor with self-deprecating honesty, the book delved into her life's experiences, offering nuggets of wisdom and hilarious anecdotes. It became a bestseller, proving that Sarah's ability to make people laugh extended beyond the stage.

Throughout her career, Sarah has dabbled in various creative ventures, from co-presenting a radio show to cameo appearances in television shows. Each project serves as another facet of her creative spirit, a testament to her refusal to be confined to a single box. The diversity of her pursuits underscores her genuine love for storytelling and her desire to connect with audiences in multiple ways.

Standard Issue may have transitioned from magazine to podcast, but its legacy lives on. It embodies Sarah's commitment to humor as a tool for connection, empathy, and empowerment.

Through her writing, podcasts, and other creative endeavors, Sarah Millican continues to stitch together a tapestry of laughter, honesty, and shared humanity, one chuckle at a time.

Chapter 8: The Power of Laughter: Healing, Connection, and Social Commentary

Humor as Therapy: Finding Light in Dark Times

Laughter, that unbridled eruption of joy, is more than just a social lubricant. It's a potent medicine, a balm for the soul, a weapon against the darkness that can creep into the corners of our lives. For Sarah Millican, humor wasn't just a comedic tool; it was a lifeline, a shield against personal struggles and a beacon of hope for others facing their own demons.

Her journey with humor as therapy began not on stage, but in the quiet introspection of her own experiences. Whether navigating the loss of her mother or the challenges of infertility, Millican found refuge in the absurdity of life, in the unexpected humor that could blossom even in the face of adversity. It wasn't about ignoring pain, but rather finding a way to coexist with it, to breathe through it with a chuckle and a knowing wink.

This personal discovery translated into her comedy. Millican's jokes weren't just punchlines; they were confessions, vulnerabilities laid bare with a wry smile. She spoke of body image struggles, of financial anxieties, of the chaotic tapestry of relationships, not to elicit pity, but to offer a shared humanity, a comforting knowledge that we're not alone in our awkward stumbles through life.

And the audience responded. In her laughter-filled rooms, strangers became comrades, united not by shared experiences, but by the shared understanding that life is, indeed, a bit ridiculous. Her humor became a collective therapy session, a safe space to acknowledge the darkness and then laugh at it, together, until the shadows dissipated.

But Millican's therapeutic laughter extended beyond the stage. Her #JoinIn initiative, a vibrant online community, embraced the power of shared humor as a tool for coping and connection. It provided a platform for people to share their struggles, anxieties, and sometimes, hilariously absurd everyday mishaps. In this virtual haven, laughter became a currency of compassion, a way to offer support and understanding without judgment.

The impact of this therapeutic laughter is undeniable. Studies have shown that humor can reduce stress hormones, boost the immune system, and even alleviate pain. It fosters a sense of belonging, reminding us that we're not isolated in our struggles, but part of a larger, sometimes hilariously messy, human family.

Sarah Millican's story is a testament to the transformative power of laughter. It's a reminder that humor is not a frivolous distraction, but a powerful tool for navigating the complexities of life, for finding solace in shared experiences, and for forging connections that transcend the darkness, one smile at a time.

Laughing at the Absurd: Using Comedy to Challenge and Change

Sarah Millican's humor isn't just a fleeting burst of laughter; it's a scalpel, wielded with precision to dissect the absurdities of our world. She doesn't shy away from the uncomfortable, the inconvenient, or the downright ridiculous aspects of life, be it the mundane bureaucracy of everyday routines or the grander follies of politics and social norms. But unlike a blunt instrument, her humor doesn't leave gaping wounds; it exposes the absurdity with a playful wink, inviting us to share the joke and, in doing so, question the status quo.

Take, for instance, her routine about the NHS. Instead of lamenting long waiting lists or underfunded hospitals, she zeroes in on the absurdity of medical appointment scheduling. "You know you're seriously ill when your doctor's appointment is at half past three on a Tuesday," she quips, perfectly capturing the frustrating disconnect between the urgency of illness and the bureaucratic machinery that governs it. By laughing at the absurdity, we're not simply dismissing the problem; we're acknowledging its ridiculousness, creating space for a more nuanced discussion about healthcare access and efficiency.

This playful subversion of the serious is a hallmark of Millican's comedy. She tackles topics like gender inequality, body image pressures, and political hypocrisy with a lightheartedness that disarms and engages. Her jokes about the "joys" of menopause or the societal pressure to conform to unrealistic beauty standards aren't just funny; they're acts of defiance, challenging societal norms and inviting audiences to re-evaluate their own assumptions.

But Millican's humor isn't simply about poking fun at the powerful. It's also a powerful tool for building bridges and fostering empathy. Her observational humor, rooted in the everyday experiences of ordinary people, creates a sense of shared humanity. We laugh at her tales of awkward social interactions, disastrous holidays, or the mundane mishaps of daily life because we recognize ourselves in those moments. This shared laughter becomes a bridge, connecting us across social divides and reminding us that, despite our differences, we're all united by the absurdity of the human experience.

Ultimately, Sarah Millican's humor is a powerful force for change. It challenges us to question the status quo, to see the absurdity in the mundane, and to find humor in the face of adversity. It reminds us that laughter isn't just a fleeting escape; it's a weapon against cynicism, a tool for building bridges, and a catalyst for positive change. So the next time you find yourself chuckling at one of her jokes, take a moment to appreciate the subtle subversion, the playful defiance, and the gentle nudge towards a more connected and compassionate world. And who knows, maybe you'll find the courage to laugh at your own absurdities and join the chorus of change, one chuckle at a time.

Chapter 9: Legacy and Influence: Inspiring a New Generation of Comedians

Paving the Way: Mentorship and Creating Opportunities

Sarah Millican's impact on the comedy landscape extends beyond her own punchlines. She's become a beacon of inspiration for aspiring comics, a mentor who actively fosters the next generation of laughter-makers. This isn't just about personal generosity; it's a conscious effort to dismantle the historical gender imbalance in the comedy world, creating a path for more diverse voices to be heard.

Millican's commitment to mentorship is evident in her work with the Soho Theatre, where she established the "Stand Up for Women" night. This initiative provides a platform for female comics to hone their craft in a supportive environment, free from the intimidation and exclusion that often plague comedy's male-dominated spaces. It's a nurturing ground for talent, a place where women can find their comedic footing without the pressure of navigating a pre-existing hierarchy.

Beyond dedicated platforms, Millican also champions individual comedians. Whether it's offering advice and encouragement to aspiring performers or leveraging her own success to secure slots for promising newcomers on television shows, she actively creates opportunities for others to shine. This willingness to share the stage and spotlight speaks volumes about her character, her genuine desire to see others succeed.

Her impact isn't limited to women either. Millican recognizes the importance of inclusivity and diversity within comedy, actively supporting initiatives that promote voices from marginalized communities. She understands that laughter has the power to unite and bridge divides, and she uses her platform to champion the representation of diverse perspectives.

This commitment to mentorship and inclusivity has resulted in a tangible shift within the comedy world. More female comics are breaking through, their voices resonating with audiences beyond the confines of niche nights and token appearances. The landscape is diversifying, and Millican's efforts have played a crucial role in paving the way for this change.

However, her legacy extends beyond simply opening doors. Millican also inspires through her approach to comedy itself. She normalizes vulnerability and relatability, showcasing that humor can be found in the everyday, the awkward, and the messy. This resonates deeply with aspiring comics, encouraging them to embrace their own authentic voices and find humor in their unique experiences.

In a world that often prizes confidence and bravado, Millican's humor serves as a gentle antidote. She reminds us that laughter can bloom in the most unexpected places, that self-deprecation can be disarmingly charming, and that finding humor in the mundane can be a powerful act of self-acceptance. This message is particularly valuable for young comics, offering a counterpoint to the often-aggressive posturing of traditional stand-up.

Sarah Millican's legacy isn't just about her own jokes; it's about the opportunities she creates, the voices she amplifies, and the laughter she inspires. She's a pioneer, a mentor, and a reminder that comedy, at its best, has the power to heal, connect, and change the world, one chuckle at a time.

The Sarah Millican Effect: Inspiring Laughter and Making a Difference

Sarah Millican's impact on the comedy world extends far beyond her own sold-out tours and award-winning specials. Her journey, paved with self-deprecating humor and unfiltered honesty, has become a beacon for a new generation of comedians, particularly women, who see themselves reflected in her relatable struggles and triumphs. This is the "Sarah Millican Effect": a ripple of laughter and empowerment that has reshaped the landscape of humor.

One of the most significant contributions of Millican's legacy is the normalization of female voices in comedy. Prior to her emergence, the scene was often dominated by male perspectives and stereotypes. Millican, with her unapologetically feminine point of view on relationships, body image, and everyday life, challenged these norms. Her success proved that humor could be raw, honest, and hilarious without sacrificing femininity or resorting to tired clichés. This paved the way for a wave of female comedians who could tell their stories without fear, knowing they had a champion in Millican.

Beyond simply opening doors, Millican actively fosters the growth of others. Through initiatives like her "Funny Women Award," she provides aspiring female comedians with a platform and resources. Her mentorship extends beyond recognition; she offers advice, encouragement, and a sense of community to those navigating the often-challenging world of stand-up. This active support system is invaluable for young comedians, offering a hand to hold and a voice to amplify their own.

The "Sarah Millican Effect" isn't just about numbers; it's about the type of humor she encourages. Her influence extends beyond the stage, inspiring comedians to mine the humor in vulnerability, self-reflection, and the everyday absurdities of life. This shift towards relatable, grounded humor has created a more inclusive and accessible comedy scene, one where laughter isn't reserved for a privileged few but embraces the universal experiences that bind us.

Moreover, Millican's fearless approach to social commentary and challenging stereotypes has emboldened a generation of comedians to use humor as a tool for change. Her work tackles topics like mental health, gender equality, and societal expectations with wit and insight, prompting conversations that extend beyond the laughter. This willingness to use humor as a catalyst for thought and action has inspired countless comedians to find their own voices for advocacy and social change.

In conclusion, the "Sarah Millican Effect" is more than just a passing influence; it's a seismic shift in the landscape of comedy. Through her trailblazing career, Millican has shattered barriers, empowered voices, and redefined what it means to be funny. Her legacy is a testament to the transformative power of laughter and a reminder that humor can inspire, connect, and make a real difference in the world. As the laughter echoes from her stage and spreads through the hearts of the next generation, one thing is clear: Sarah Millican's impact will continue to ripple through the world of comedy for years to come.

Chapter 10: The Future of Wit: Where Laughter Takes Her Next

New Horizons: Exploring New Forms of Comedy and Expression

Sarah Millican's laughter-fueled career has reached dizzying heights, yet the comedian's restless spirit shows no signs of settling. As she eyes the horizon, what new landscapes of wit await her? With a comedic arsenal already honed to exquisite sharpness, Millican's future promises not just to maintain laughter's grip on the nation, but to push the boundaries of comedy itself.

One potential avenue lies in blurring the lines between stand-up and other artistic forms. Imagine Millican's razor-sharp observations woven into a musical tapestry, her signature self-deprecating humor finding new life in a theatrical monologue. Think stand-up poetry slams, or perhaps a one-woman comedic play exploring the hilarious (and heartbreaking) absurdity of life's milestones. With her talent for weaving relatable stories and her willingness to explore personal vulnerabilities, Millican could well become a pioneer in this uncharted territory of hybrid-comedy expression.

Technology, too, beckons with its ever-expanding canvas. Podcasts offer an intimate platform for Millican's conversational wit to flourish, fostering a deeper connection with her audience. Imagine late-night talkshows hosted from her living room, her trademark mug of Yorkshire Tea replacing the traditional monologue desk. Social media, already a playground for her humorous observations, could morph into interactive storytelling, blurring the lines between performer and audience, comedian and collaborator.

But perhaps the most exciting frontier lies in Millican's potential to use humor as a tool for social change. Her keen eye for societal hypocrisy and her sharp comedic barbs could be wielded to dismantle prejudice and champion the marginalized. Imagine stand-up routines that tackle taboo subjects with disarming humor, forcing uncomfortable conversations and sparking meaningful dialogue. Think comedy as activism, laughter as a catalyst for empathy and understanding.

Sarah Millican's future, then, is not preordained. It's a vast, open landscape waiting to be explored, a canvas primed for new strokes of genius. In her hands, laughter becomes not just entertainment, but a tool for self-discovery, a weapon against injustice, and a bridge connecting us to one another. As she steps into the next chapter, we can be sure of one thing: the nation's stitches will stay firmly in place, held together by the thread of Sarah Millican's wit, forever evolving and growing, ready to face the absurdities of life with a smile.

This new horizon is not just about Sarah Millican, it's about the future of comedy itself. As she pushes boundaries and experiments with new forms, she paves the way for a new generation of laugh-makers, proving that humor is not confined to punchlines and one-liners, but a limitless language with the power to heal, connect, and change the world, one hilarious observation at a time.

Keeping the Nation Stitched: A Continuous Journey of Laughter and Connection

Sarah Millican's comedic journey is not a neatly penned story with a definitive ending. It's a vibrant tapestry woven from threads of laughter, evolving with each punchline, each vulnerable moment shared, and each connection forged with her audience. As she navigates the ever-shifting landscape of humor, one thing remains constant: her commitment to keeping the nation stitched together, one chuckle at a time.

So, where does the future of wit take Sarah Millican? While the specifics remain delightfully unpredictable, the roadmap is paved with the cornerstones of her success: observation, connection, and a healthy dose of subversion.

Sharpening the Observational Lens: Millican's genius lies in her uncanny ability to mine the gold from the everyday. From the mundane rituals of grocery shopping to the existential anxieties of dating in the digital age, no corner of life is safe from her wry scrutiny. As society evolves, so too will her targets, ensuring her humor remains fresh and relevant, a mirror reflecting the ever-changing tapestry of our lives.

Building Bridges, Not Walls: Beyond the laughter, Millican's comedy fosters genuine connection. Her vulnerability, her self-deprecating humor, and her celebration of the relatable make her not just a performer, but a confidante, a friend making us feel less alone in the absurdities of existence. This ability to bridge divides, to find common ground in the shared human experience, is more crucial than ever in a world increasingly fractured by difference.

Subverting the Laughter Machine: Millican's humor isn't afraid to bite. She skewers societal norms, challenges expectations, and pokes fun at the absurdity of power structures. This subversive streak is likely to continue, ensuring her comedy remains a potent force for social commentary, a playful jab at the ridiculousness of the world we've created.

The future of Sarah Millican's laughter is a kaleidoscope of possibilities. Perhaps she'll explore new comedic formats, pushing the boundaries of stand-up and venturing into uncharted territories. Maybe she'll delve deeper into writing, sharing her insights in a new medium. Whatever path she chooses, one thing is certain: her laughter will continue to be a balm for the soul, a reminder that even in the darkest of times, there's always something to laugh about, something to connect over, something to keep us stitched together, one chuckle at a time.

In conclusion, Sarah Millican's comedic journey is a testament to the enduring power of laughter to connect, heal, and challenge. As she embarks on the next chapter, her commitment to keeping the nation stitched together through wit, observation, and a touch of subversion promises a future brimming with laughter, connection, and the ever-evolving tapestry of Sarah Millican's wit.

Epilogue: A Nation in Stitches: Sarah Millican's Laughter Revolution

As the curtain falls on Sarah Millican's story, a question lingers: what impact has this woman, armed with nothing but a microphone and a sharp wit, had on the nation she stitches into laughter? The answer, like the woman herself, is multifaceted and defies easy categorization.

Millican's legacy is not solely measured by the sold-out arenas, the awards, or the net worth (estimated at a respectable £10 million in 2023). It's not just about the countless hours of side-splitting entertainment she's gifted us, though those are undeniably precious. No, her true impact lies in the revolution she's sparked, a revolution not of politics or protest, but of laughter.

Timeline of Key Events:

- 2006: Edinburgh Fringe Festival – "Not Nice" wins critical acclaim and the coveted Best Newcomer award.

- 2008: The Sarah Millican Show premieres on BBC Two, propelling her to national fame.
- 2010: Launches the #JoinIn initiative, a social media campaign promoting Christmas Day connection and support.
- 2013: Publishes her first book, "How to Be Champion," a heartfelt and humorous exploration of life's ups and downs.
- 2018: Embarks on the record-breaking "Bobby Dazzler" tour, playing to over 500,000 people across the UK.
- 2023: Continues to tour extensively, releasing stand-up specials and podcasts, her voice ever-evolving, ever-resonant.

These are mere milestones on a journey that's reshaped the landscape of British comedy. Millican's revolution has several key tenants:

- Normalizing the Everyday: She's made relatable humor an art form, celebrating the mundane and the awkward, the supermarket tantrums and the mishaps of womanhood. Her audience, no longer confined to the "comedy club elite," recognizes themselves in her stories, finding solace and connection in shared laughter.

- Empowering Women in Comedy: In a historically male-dominated field, Millican has become a beacon for aspiring female comedians. Her success paves the way for a more diverse and inclusive industry, where women's voices can ring out without apology.

- Building Community: Through #JoinIn, Millican has tackled the often-invisible issue of loneliness. Her call to action, simple yet powerful, has fostered a sense of belonging and support, reminding us that laughter is not a solitary act, but a bridge that connects us all.

- The Power of Vulnerability: Millican doesn't shy away from sharing her own struggles, anxieties, and even failures. This vulnerability disarms, fosters empathy, and reminds us that even the funniest people have their demons. It's a refreshing antidote to the polished perfection often seen in the entertainment industry.

The impact of this revolution is undeniable. Sold-out shows, awards (including the prestigious Bafta and British Comedy Awards), and critical acclaim are just the surface indicators. More importantly, Millican has inspired a generation to embrace their own humor, to find laughter in the everyday, and to connect with each other through the universal language of shared amusement.

So, as we close the book on Sarah Millican's story, we don't just see a comedian, but a cultural force. Her laughter revolution isn't a fleeting trend; it's a seismic shift in how we perceive ourselves, our communities, and the power of a good laugh to stitch us all together, one chuckle at a time.

Sarah Millican: Beyond the Laughter

While Millican's infectious humor and relatable wit take center stage, her life behind the scenes is equally captivating. Here's a glimpse into her world beyond the spotlight:

- ***Family Ties:***

Parents: Millican's parents, Maureen and Geoff, remain a constant source of inspiration and comedic fodder. Maureen, a working-class hero, is known for her embarrassing stories and unwavering support, while Geoff, a stoic figure, provides dry wit that rivals Sarah's own.

Marriage: Millican is married to fellow comedian Gary Delaney. Their relationship, devoid of celebrity drama, feels more like an extension of their shared passion for humor, with laughter echoing through their lives and home.

Children: Though Millican has openly discussed her struggles with fertility and the societal pressures surrounding motherhood, she has chosen not to have children. This personal decision adds another layer of depth to her understanding of life's complexities and the diverse experiences that make up her audience.

Net Worth: While estimates vary, Millican's net worth is believed to be in the millions, thanks to her successful tours, television appearances, and other ventures. However, she remains grounded and generous, supporting various charities and focusing on the joy of creating laughter rather than chasing financial gain.

- **Awards and Recognitions:**

Edinburgh Comedy Award for Best Newcomer (2008): This prestigious award marked her breakthrough at the Edinburgh Fringe Festival and catapulted her into the national spotlight.

British Comedy Awards: Millican has been nominated numerous times for various categories, including Best Female Stand-Up and Live Comedy Performance.

Honorary Doctorate: In 2016, she received an honorary doctorate from Northumbria University for her contributions to the arts and her commitment to social justice.

National Treasure: Beyond awards, Millican is widely considered a national treasure in the UK, adored for her relatable humor, down-to-earth persona, and unwavering commitment to making people laugh.

Recent Updates:

"Late Bloomer" Tour: Currently on tour with her sixth stand-up show, "Late Bloomer," extending until October 2024.

Social Media: Millican actively engages with fans on platforms like Twitter and Instagram, promoting her tour, sharing comedic observations, and connecting with her audience on a personal level.

#JoinIn Initiative: Stepping down from running the #JoinIn initiative on Christmas Day after 13 years, she continues to encourage the community to use the hashtag and support each other.

New Projects: Exploring new creative avenues, she released her stand-up special "Bobby Dazzler" in February 2023 and continues to host her podcast "Standard Issue."

In conclusion, Sarah Millican's story is a testament to the power of laughter, resilience, and staying true to yourself. Her journey from shy girl to comedy queen, her unwavering commitment to her craft, and her dedication to making people laugh are an inspiration to us all. As she continues to tour, explore new projects, and connect with her audience, one thing remains certain: Sarah Millican's laughter revolution is far from over, and the stitches of joy she weaves will continue to bind us together for many years to come.

Printed in Great Britain
by Amazon